Still Standing

by Barbara Gannett

 HOUGHTON MIFFLIN   BOSTON

During the 1989 San Francisco earthquake, this roadway collapsed.

The Day the Earth Shook

On October 17, 1989, San Francisco began to shake. For fifteen seconds, the earth rocked. Roads cracked. Bridges collapsed. An earthquake had struck this California city.

Some buildings fell. Others swayed, but after the quake was over, they were still standing. What made the earth quake? Why did some buildings crumble? Why did others make it through?

What Is an Earthquake?

Earthquakes happen in many places all around the world. An earthquake is usually caused because parts of Earth's crust push each other. This area is called a fault. Stress builds up. The rocks can even bend. Suddenly, parts of Earth's crust slide past each other. Big sections of rock under Earth's surface move. When the crust moves like this, the ground shakes. This is an earthquake.

The San Andreas Fault in California is a place where two parts of the Earth's crust rub together.

Earthquake Prediction

People can't prevent earthquakes. They can't even tell when earthquakes will come. They can learn from them though.

By studying earthquake damage, scientists are learning about the inside of the earth. They are also learning how to build safer buildings.

This building suffered damage in a 2001 earthquake that hit Olympia, Washington.

Buildings in Turkey fell during a 1999 earthquake.

Learning from Earthquakes

Scientists look at the damage after an earthquake. What keeps a building safe? What makes a building fall?

Sometimes buildings fall because of the materials used to make them. Buildings made of mud, bricks, or even concrete can crumble and fall in earthquakes. Buildings made of wood and steel can move with the shaking ground. This helps them stay up.

Why Buildings Fall

Sometimes buildings fall because of where they are built. If a building is built where the ground cracks, it will often fall down. If a structure is built on loose wet soil, the earthquake can cause the soil to act like quicksand. A building might start to sink, and then collapse.

This building and parking lot were damaged after an earthquake in Oakland, California.

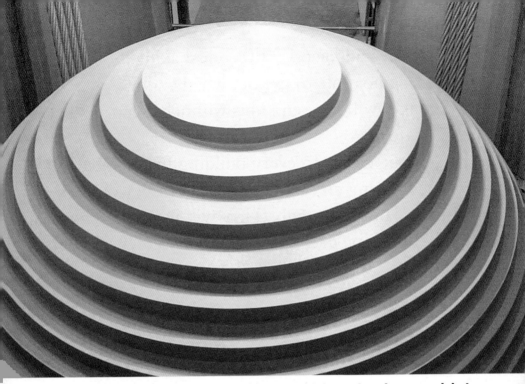

This damper protects the tallest building in the world, in Taiwan, from high winds and earthquakes.

Special Types of Buildings

Scientists are learning how to design buildings that will be more likely to stay in one piece in an earthquake. "Dampers," like giant shock absorbers, have been put in some buildings. They are called dampers because the machine absorbs or dampens some of the earthquake's shaking vibrations.

No one can keep Earth from shaking. Someday it might be possible to predict when and where earthquakes will happen. This will help keep people safe.

No one can keep every building from being damaged during an earthquake. Scientists will learn from the damage though. They will make structures better. This way, more people will be safe during an earthquake and there will be less damage.

Seattle, Washington, after an earthquake in 2001